TEACHING THE 4CS WITH TECHNOLOGY

How do I use 21st century tools to teach 21st century skills?

Stephanie
SMITH BUDHAI

Laura
MCLAUGHLIN TADDEI

ASCD   Alexandria, VA USA

ASCD®
Website: www.ascd.org
E-mail: books@ascd.org

ASCD | arias™
www.ascdarias.org

PAPERBACK ISBN: 978-1-4166-2149-2   ASCD product # SF116038

Also available as an e-book (see Books in Print for the ISBNs).

Library of Congress Cataloging-in-Publication Data

Names: Budhai, Stephanie Smith. | Taddei, Laura McLaughlin.
Title: Fostering the 4Cs with technology : how can I leverage technology to teach 21st century skills? / Stephanie Smith Budhai, Laura McLaughlin Taddei.
Description: Alexandria, Virginia : ASCD, [2015] | Includes bibliographical references.
Identifiers: LCCN 2015032884 | ISBN 9781416621492 (pbk. : alk. paper)
Subjects: LCSH: Educational technology. | Critical thinking--Study and teaching. | Creativity--Study and teaching.

Classification: LCC LB1028.3 .B83 2015 | DDC 371.33--dc23 LC record available at http://lccn.loc.gov/2015032884

24 23 22 21 20 19 18 17 16 15   1 2 3 4 5 6 7 8 9 10

TEACHING THE 4CS WITH TECHNOLOGY

How do I use 21st century tools to teach 21st century skills?

Building 21st Century Skills Through Technology 1

Critical Thinking: Interdisciplinary
Inquiry-Based Learning 5

Communication: Videos, Wikis, Blogs,
and Social Media 18

Collaboration: Teaming with Teachers
and Partnering with Peers 27

Creativity: Encouraging Innovation and Invention 35

Encore 47

References 53

Related Resources 56

About the Authors 57

Want to earn a free ASCD Arias e-book?
Your opinion counts! Please take 2–3 minutes to give
us your feedback on this publication. All survey
respondents will be entered into a drawing to
win an ASCD Arias e-book.

Please visit
www.ascd.org/ariasfeedback

Thank you!

Building 21st Century Skills Through Technology

The 4Cs—critical thinking, communication, collaboration, and creativity—are the basic skills all students need in the 21st century (National Education Association, 2014). Additionally, technology is constantly emerging around us, and expected to be part of every student's learning experience. This book provides practical suggestions and ideas to leverage the use of technology to guide students toward thinking critically about what they are learning, building interpersonal communication skills, working more effectively with teams, and creating and innovating new ideas, concepts, and products.

We decided to write this book because we are striving to be 21st century educators who prepare our students to live and work in a global society. We have found through trial and error how technology creates environments where students can develop critical thinking, communication, collaboration, and creativity skills. Rosefsky Saavedra and Opfer (2012) urged:

> . . . if we believe 21st century skills are the key to solving economic, civic, and global challenges and to engaging effectively in those spheres, then we must act upon the belief

that using those skills to overhaul our education systems is possible. (p. 12)

We know the impact and transformational experience technology brings, but it is important to look at the use of technology in the classroom by asking ourselves "What do we want students to learn?", and after we have the objective, "How can technology transform the learning experience and foster the 4Cs?" Asking these questions in this way keeps the focus on *learning* and not on technology integration.

This book provides specific ways to meet the 4Cs through the use of technology. It is useful for teachers, teacher educators, instructional coaches, technology integration specialists, and undergraduate and graduate students. These generalized instructional best practices can be implemented in a variety of classroom settings, from preK through grade 12.

Each section includes suggestions to support best practices for each skill, examples of ways technology can be integrated, and practical tips and reflective questions to consider with teachers and administrators. The Encore section provides practical and relevant takeaways. We hope to collect stories from those who want to share their own integration of technology and how this connects to the 4Cs, so the Encore includes a link to a short survey where you can help us keep the conversation going.

We also provide specific ways to move from the substitution stage to the redefinition stage of technology integration, guided by the SAMR (Substitution-

Augmentation-Modification-Redefinition) framework. The SAMR framework serves as a support for teachers and administrators as they examine their use of technology (Puentedura, 2009).

There are four stages to the SAMR framework: Substitution-Augmentation-Modification-Redefinition. During the **substitution** stage, technology replaces a tool to carry out the same function, but it does not change the learning environment. For example, a washing machine is a technology tool that people substitute for washing clothes by hand. The hand and washing machine serve the same function; most people substitute the washing machine for their hands to make the process more efficient. In the school setting, students use word processing programs to draft academic writing, as opposed to pencil and paper. These are both technology integration at the substitution level.

The **augmentation** stage occurs when technology contributes to a change in the learning environment to improve the functionality of the learning experience. Allowing students to save their documents automatically to the cloud, as opposed to manually saving them, is an example of augmentation. The functionality of saving work has changed.

The **modification** stage leads to the integration of technology that causes a significant change in the learning environment and allows educators to redesign learning tasks in new and meaningful ways. This is the first step of using technology to alter learning tasks and experiences. Imagine that a history assignment called for students to create a timeline of the last century, highlighting one major event each decade. Normally, students would present their work using a piece of paper and pencil by drawing the timeline and writing the events on the paper, or using a computer to type their timeline. An example of modifying this task with technology could include requiring students to create a virtual timeline using a multimedia application such as Timetoast. This task would also require them to embed a brief summary of the event in the timeline, which could be assessed by clicking the title as well as a function for peers to comment via the Internet.

The redefinition stage occurs when technology redefines learning and results in innovative teaching and learning environments that would not have been possible without the integration of technology. Learning activities at this level use multiple technology tools including the ability to work on projects and documents simultaneously with peers, collaborating with people around the world, and creating digital and tangible projects infused with technology.

Regardless of the SAMR level, the use of technology should be purposeful and enhance learning. Do not use technology because it is there. No matter how innovative technology may be, if it is not positively influencing learning goals, then it should not be used (Johnson, 2013). We mention many different tools and apps within our examples of technology integration, but the tool or app is not what determines the level of function; it is how this tool or app is used (Green, 2014). If someone chooses not to use the features of a particular app or tool, then the level of integration would remain at a basic level (Green, 2014). For this reason, many of our suggestions can be used with a variety of tools and at a variety of SAMR levels.

The resources available in this text will help teachers

- Integrate technology into a wide range of subject areas and grade levels for all types of technology set-ups.
- Identify ways students can think critically, communicate with one another, collaborate as teams, and be creative with the use of technology.
- Provide suggestions of technology ideas along the SAMR ladder beyond substitution.
- Develop a toolkit of media and virtual website resources.

Critical Thinking: Interdisciplinary Inquiry-Based Learning

The important thing is not to stop questioning.
—Albert Einstein

Critical thinking is at the crux of learning and developing 21st century skills. According to the Partnership for 21st Century Learning, while once reserved for gifted students, critical thinking and problem-solving skills are now important for all students to master (National Education Association, 2014). Critical thinking requires students to analyze, synthesize, and evaluate concepts and constructs presented in a learning unit (Bloom, 1956). This section presents ways to incorporate activities that build critical thinking skills through the use of learning technologies with an emphasis on inquiry-based learning activities.

The International Society for Technology in Education (ISTE, 2007) includes critical thinking, problem solving, and decision making as one of six standards for students. Students need opportunities to "plan and conduct research, manage projects, solve problems, and make informed decisions using appropriate digital tools and resources" (ISTE, 2007). Teachers need to find the best use of technology to help students meet these goals. Bain (n.d) provided the following advice:

> Ideally, computers can help us foster the accomplishment of the highest learning objectives we have for our students: the ability to think critically and creatively, to reason, to use our disciplinary approaches to information, to learn and to want to learn independently of any formal instruction, and to work collaboratively in solving important problems.

Problem-based inquiry learning is a proven strategy to help engage students in critical thinking, "which focuses on spontaneity, collaboration, and flexible problem-solving skills" (Pi-Hsia et al., 2014, p. 316). Technology has enhanced the use of applying problem-based inquiry learning to a variety of situations and meeting the needs of diverse learners. The use of ubiquitous tools has created an environment where learning can occur outside of the classroom and continue even after the course or school day ends. When students have opportunities to think about what they are learning in a variety of contexts, this also increases their understanding. Integrating technology and asking students to demonstrate their learning through the use of technology provides alternative assessments where teachers can see how they have learned and how they are thinking about what they learned. As students become more engaged and interested in what they are learning, thinking critically will come more naturally.

Practical Tips to Meet the 21st Century Skill of Critical Thinking Using Technology

Critical thinking involves students making decisions, reasoning, and problem solving while learning. In our digital society, students have access to a plethora of information and can find out almost anything they want to know. However, building on this knowledge and expanding on what students already know requires critical thinking (MacKnight, 2000). How can teachers help students to think critically? In what ways can technology be used to foster higher-level thinking and deeper learning?

Bloom's taxonomy can serve as a guide to teachers when planning for these higher-level thinking opportunities. To ensure their students are moving toward levels IV, V, and VI of analyzing, synthesizing, and evaluating (Bloom's Taxonomy, n.d.), teachers can intentionally create questions, assignments, and prompts that challenge students to reach each level. Teachers can also model higher-level thinking in their own responses to students by reasoning and discussing how they solve problems and how they think about their own thinking (metacognition). Explicitly telling students that you want them to think of themselves as thinkers is important. Some tools teachers currently use to encourage metacognition include pre-assessments, muddiest points, self-assessments, reflective journals, and metacognition logs (Chick, n.d.). How can technology facilitate this important 21st century skill of critical thinking? According to the Partnership for 21st Century Learning Framework, critical thinking is broken up into subskills. Our goal is to provide technology strategies for these subskills with suggestions on how to encourage our students to be critical thinkers not only when they are students, but for life.

Subskill: Reason Effectively

This subskill requires students to use various types of reasoning as appropriate to the situation. The Common Core State Standards consider students who are college and career ready to possess the ability to reason effectively (Common Core State Standards Initiative, 2015). Students can demonstrate their reasoning skills by critiquing and discussing something they have read and providing evidence and sources to back up their arguments. Regarding technology, students who reason effectively can take something they have learned online and synthesize the information with something they have learned offline. When students are able to reason effectively, they also strive to understand diverse perspectives and cultures (Common Core State Standards

Initiative, 2015). Technology provides ways to transform or enhance instruction so students have opportunities to practice and demonstrate effective reasoning. Here are some specific strategies to use in the classroom along with the SAMR level for each strategy:

Tech strategy: Research information online (SAMR level: Augmentation). Asking students to research online provides opportunities to reason effectively because they have to decide what information to use and why. Encourage students to provide sources to support their reasoning. This evidence also supports their ability to think critically. According to the Common Core standards, as early as kindergarten, students should have opportunities to participate in shared or individual research. At this early level, the teacher may conduct research with the students about butterflies as they learn about the life cycle. As they continue on in school, these research projects can become more intense and involved. By high school, students are expected to

- "Conduct short as well as more sustained research projects to answer a question (including a self-generated question) or solve a problem; narrow or broaden the inquiry when appropriate; synthesize multiple sources on the subject, demonstrating understanding of the subject under investigation" (CCSS-ELA Writing W.11-12.7).
- Choose a problem to solve. Within this assignment, they will be expected to use multiple sources, synthesize this information, and present the information to others.

Here are some other practical augmentation tech strategies to support reasoning effectively:

- Create a space online where students can view and share resources that support their ideas or views on the course topic.
- Ask open-ended and productive questions to guide the discussion on online discussion boards.
- Create a survey on Google Forms, and ask students to answer reflective questions about a classroom experience.
- Encourage the use of Google Docs so students can save work, share work, and have opportunities to take part in reviewing and providing feedback to peers.
- Provide students with digital media, videos, and notes before class to review so when they come to class, they will be more prepared to critically discuss and practice reasoning.

Tech strategy: Use teacher-created blogs (SAMR level: Modification). Blogs provide teachers with opportunities to create and write, modifying instruction and leading to a significant change in the teaching and learning environment. In fact, Richardson (2010) described the use of blogs as "a constructivist tool for learning" (p. 26). Constructivism allows learners to have hands-on experiences and opportunities to make sense of their learning. When students reason, they are also making sense of their thinking and then sharing these thoughts with others. Blogs allow the content to be shared to a larger audience through the Internet. They also provide an archive of learning among teachers and students, "facilitating all sorts of reflection and metacognitive analysis that was previously much more cumbersome" (Richardson, 2010, p. 27). Evidence of students' abilities to reason effectively can be easily shared and stored for assessment and evaluation within this blog—providing opportunities to reflect and improve on teaching and learning.

Here are some other practical modification tech strategies to support reasoning effectively:

- Use voice-recorded technology (e.g., VoiceThread) and ask students to record their thoughts to specific instructor-created prompts, listen to their classmates' responses, and comment on their classmates' and teachers' responses.
- Incorporate virtual tours and live webcams into your teaching so students can gain background knowledge and experiences in places they might not have visited.
- Use games to teach students to reason effectively.

Tech strategy: Share student-created digital media presentation on social media (SAMR level: Redefinition). When students are given opportunities to create something new, they engage in effective reasoning when they decide on their topic, gather research, synthesize the information, and then create a presentation to share with others. According to the Common Core State Standards, students should "integrate visual information (e.g., in charts, graphs, photographs, videos, or maps) with other information in print and digital texts" (CCSS.ELA-LITERACY.RH.6-8.7). When students have opportunities to share their presentations online (using a wiki, social media, or website), the teaching and learning environment is redefined. Students can interact with others across the country, and discuss and defend their project through online discussions. Students can also view others' digital presentations they would not have had access to without technology.

Here are some other practical redefinition tech strategies to support reasoning effectively. Ask students to

- Create their own video, blog, or digital story to support their reasoning.
- Create something using digital games (e.g., Minecraft), and then record the games and reflect on what was created.
- Use Google Docs and Google Hangouts to work on a group project and then share their project with the online community via social media.
- Use Skype within the classroom so they can interact with others in a different location or from a different culture.
- Create an e-portfolio demonstrating their learning. This e-portfolio should include artifacts like sample work, text, audio, video, and pictures.

Subskill: Use Systems Thinking

Students also need to be able to analyze how parts of a whole interact with each other and then how these systems work within a complex system. Engaging students as early as preschool in practicing systems thinking has proven to be beneficial (Clark, 2014). The sooner teachers help students see the big picture and how things depend on each other, the more connections they will make and the greater the learning. It's important for students to be able to think about thinking (metacognition), and systems thinking involves reflection, making connections, and being a self-directed learner. The Partnership for 21st Century Learning described using tools such as behavior-over-time charts, causal loops, and stocks and flows to help children develop systems thinking (Clark, 2014). These tools provide students with visuals of how to think critically. The children envision and learn about change, variables, and how events affect an entire system. Technology can enhance and even transform how you teach and how children learn this 21st century critical thinking skill. Here are some specific strategies to use in the classroom along with the SAMR level for each strategy:

Tech strategy: Use voice-recorded reflections of systems change (SAMR level: Augmentation). Reflections are an integral part of teaching and learning about systems change. Having the ability to go back and listen to their reflections creates opportunities for students to reflect and understand their thinking. VoiceThread is a tool that is easy to use and allows students to share their reflections with others and even invite others to respond to their reflections. This strategy can be used for any topic that involves change over time. For example, if students plant seeds, they can record their reflections every day and describe in words what they see, how things are different, and why they think these changes are happening. They can also observe their classmates' plants, compare and describe the differences using the voice-recorded tool.

Here are some other practical augmentation tech strategies to support systems thinking:

- Provide online resources regarding systems and how they work. For example, students may better understand a specific ecosystem if they can see it and visualize it with pictures and videos. Suggested tools include YouTube, iTunes U, Keynote, PowerPoint, and Prezi.
- Send home a list to families of online games (e.g., Minecraft, SimCity, Civilization, and Gamestar Mechanic) that support systems thinking.
- Ask students to use an online journal or blog to record thoughts about systems thinking. Possible tools include Edublogs, Kidblog, Penzu, Notability, and Evernote.
- Integrate an online discussion on systems thinking through the course management system, Google Apps for Education, or Wikispaces.
- Suggest that students use graphic organizers. A sample list of available online graphic organizers can be found here: www.educatorstechnology.com/2012/02/list-of-free-graphic-organizers-for.html?m=1. Students can use Popplet or Educreations.

Tech strategy: Use mobile apps to support systems thinking (SAMR level: Modification). Mobile apps provide 24/7 learning opportunities and are also "seen as enablers of more personalized learning" ("Mobile Learning," 2013, p. 8). Given that there are numerous apps to choose from, students may benefit when they are allowed to use the app of their choice. For example, in a 5th grade social studies class, students can use any app or digital tool to create a visual (audio, graphics, or video) to describe the government, including the parts of the government and how it works. In a 2nd grade science class, students can record the weather using a mobile app (take pictures each day with a cell phone, record video using an iPad, etc.) and evaluate how weather affects their daily lives. These kind of modified learning opportunities allow students to be more creative as well as provide documentation to demonstrate learning and to reflect on their learning.

Here are some other practical modification tech strategies to support systems thinking:

- Provide students with the opportunities to engage in virtual labs to explore issues of sustainability, and resource allocation. Use Google Earth to look deeply at different parts of the world through an environmental perspective.
- Allow students to explore games that involve robotics and computational thinking where they can build and create such as eTextiles, also known as wearables (www.ccm.ece.vt.edu:8088/etextiles/), Scratch (https://scratch.mit.edu), and ABCya.com.
- Integrate age appropriate mobile apps either by allowing students to choose an app from a list of suggested apps or downloading apps on tablets for students to choose. A sample list of mobile apps to

promote critical thinking can be found here: http://
tinyurl.com/4Csmobileapps.

**Tech strategy: Create a system—Choose your topic
and technology tool (SAMR level: Redefinition).** Providing students with an opportunity to create a new system and
share their system using technology encourages higher-level
thinking and deeper learning. When students are given
opportunities to create something new they are interested
in, learning can be redefined. A survey of educators and
students revealed "children are more likely to have an interest in science, technology, engineering, and math when the
classrooms they are in incorporate personalized learning
strategies, digital technology, and social media" ("Personalized Learning," 2012, p. 10). Allowing students to choose a
topic and the technology tool to demonstrate their learning
may increase their motivation to learn. Teachers can provide
students with a list of possible tools, and if students are using
a tool that is not on the list, the teacher should review the
tool to make sure it is appropriate to use.

Here are some other practical redefinition tech strategies to support systems thinking:

- Encourage students to engage in a global issue, like
  climate change. They can engage via social media, blogs,
  service groups, and other online forums. Have them
  exhibit their real engagement through a Storify of their
  Twitter engagement on a hashtag and share what they've
  learned with their fellow students.

- Ask students to create an online resource or video explaining how a problem affects the local, national, international, and global communities. Within this video, they will advocate for this cause, share their video via social media, and elicit feedback from others. Tools to use to create and edits videos are iMovie, YouTube Capture, WeVideo, Magisto, and Storyboard That.

- Share online resources with families and students that encourage students to create and think about systems thinking. For example, PBS kids created an online world to encourage systems thinking in young children (http://pbskids.org/kartkingdom). This online game will also allow players to play online and interact with other players around the world.

Reflection Questions for Individual or Group Discussion with Teachers

- In what ways have you used technology to influence your students' critical thinking skills?

- What is one thing you would like to try in your classroom but have not had an opportunity to do yet regarding critical thinking and technology?

- What kind of support do you have or need when it comes to trying something new in your classroom?

- In what ways do your students have opportunities to practice and demonstrate 21st century skills such as critical thinking, problem solving, and decision making?

- How can you collaborate with your colleagues and administrators to use technology to meet the 21st century skill of critical thinking?

Communication: Videos, Wikis, Blogs, and Social Media

You can have brilliant ideas, but if you can't get them across, your ideas won't get you anywhere.

—Lee Iacocca

Students need opportunities to develop effective communication skills in the 21st century. The digital generation is inundated with technology that makes teaching communication skills critical (National Education Association, 2014). When students have opportunities to interact and communicate using technology, teaching and learning is enhanced (Frey, Fisher, & Gonzalez, 2013). Because students today are digital and social learners, building competence in online technology is a critical communication skill for them as 21st century learners. Using tools such as videos, wikis, blogs, and social media can transform learning and capture the interest of students. These emerging technology tools used within programs provide a way for teaching and learning to become a 24/7 experience (Moczygemba, 2014).

The ISTE standards for students include communicating through digital media and interacting with peers and others in a variety of online formats. In addition, students are expected to "develop cultural understanding and global awareness by engaging with learners of other cultures" (ISTE, 2007). Additionally, the Common Core State Standards seek to prepare students who

> employ technology thoughtfully to enhance their reading, writing, speaking, listening, and language use. They tailor their searches online to acquire useful information efficiently, and they integrate what they learn using technology with what they learn offline. They are familiar with the strengths and limitations of various technological tools and mediums and can select and use those best suited to their communication goals. (National Governors Association Center for Best Practices & Council of Chief State School Officers, 2010, p. 7)

Ubiquitous tools such as videos, wikis, blogs, and social media enable students to communicate information and ideas both in the classroom and outside of the classroom setting.

Practical Tips to Meet the 21st Century Skill of Communication Using Technology

The P21 Framework (Partnership for 21st Century Learning, 2015) provides the subskills students need to communicate effectively. Students need opportunities to demonstrate their ability to articulate, listen, persuade, and motivate. Another important component of the P21 Framework for communication is ensuring students can communicate in diverse environments. An additional communication goal for a 21st century learner involves possessing social skills (Luterbach & Brown, 2011). Providing students with opportunities to work in small groups can help meet these goals. Creating an environment that is open and where discussion is the norm is also important. Teachers also need to model appropriate communication skills, and one way to do this is when they interact and engage with families. You and Richman (2014) described the importance of teacher involvement in communication plans: "Teachers are parents' most important links to their schools. Any communications plan to reach parents that fails to include a role for teachers is an incomplete plan" (p. 14). How can technology enable students and teachers to communicate and demonstrate these important subskills? Below we provide practical suggestions for using technology beyond the substitution stage to help students communicate clearly.

Subskill: Communicate Clearly

In the 21st century, students must be able to communicate widely through a broad range of mediums and modalities. Visual communication is equally important, requiring students to produce imagery, videos, pictures, and even crafting text-based communicative devices. The Partnership for 21st Century Learning (2015, p. 4) defines communicating clearly as having the ability to

- Articulate thoughts and ideas effectively using oral, written and nonverbal communication skills in a variety of forms and contexts
- Listen effectively to decipher meaning, including knowledge, values, attitudes and intentions
- Use communication for a range of purposes (e.g. to inform, instruct, motivate and persuade)
- Utilize multiple media and technologies, and know how to judge their effectiveness a priori as well as assess their impact
- Communicate effectively in diverse environments (including multi-lingual)

The Common Core standards have identified "Speaking and Listening" as a core anchor standard throughout the K–12 curriculum (Common Core State Standards Initiative, 2015). This anchor standard focuses on "comprehension and collaboration" and "presentation of knowledge and ideas." By embedding communication skills into the state curriculum, the importance of its usage for students moving forward into the 21st century is transparent. Examples of how technology can be augmented, modified, and redefined to help students develop and master 21st century communication skills follow:

Tech strategy: Use Google Apps for Education to communicate (SAMR level: Augmentation). Google Apps for Education is an excellent tool that students, teachers, and schools can use to encourage communication. It provides

24/7 support and access at no cost. When teachers use Google Apps to augment learning, and move beyond the substitution stage, they are not using it just as a word processing tool and a place to store information. Google Apps can take technology use from substitution to redefinition, but this tech strategy will focus on the augmentation stage and helping students to communicate clearly. For example, students can respond to questions related to a course topic that teachers post on Google+. In addition, a teacher can create a survey on Google Forms at the beginning of a course, and ask students questions about their background information on the topic and how they learn best. In order to build community in the classroom, questions can include a student's interests, a favorite book or song, or a quote or saying that defines them. This information can then be used once class starts to help students and teachers get to know each other. If students feel safe within their classroom setting, they will be more likely to share their ideas, listen to others, and communicate effectively. Not all students will freely share their ideas and thoughts within a classroom setting, so providing alternative ways for students to communicate using technology is good practice. Gray (2012) reiterates the importance of helping students find their voice:

> By using web tools like forums, message boards, Twitter, or other online lecture tools, teachers can help empower the less vocal students in a classroom. Many shyer students are quiet during classroom discussions not because they don't have anything

to say, but because they are scared to speak out in front of their peers.

The tools offered within Google Apps for Education certainly add another level of function and improvement to the 21st century skill of communication and communicating effectively.

Here are some other practical augmentation tech strategies to support communicating effectively:

- Use Quizlet to study and review course topics. In order for students to communicate effectively, they have to understand what they are learning first.
- Using tools such as Notability and Evernote, record notes and information and then share this information as a way to communicate.
- Create a Padlet page and ask students to communicate their thoughts on a topic, or create small groups and have each group record their ideas on their own Padlet page.

Tech strategy: Share and receive ideas through technology-driven social interactions (SAMR level: Modification). Students need opportunities to present and receive information through multiple forms of communicative interactions. Technology-driven social interactions and social media can serve as a catalyst to communicating these ideas. The Common Core State Standards spell these out at all grade levels. At the elementary level, students must be able to "Create audio recordings of stories or poems; add drawings or other visual displays to stories or recounts of experiences when appropriate to clarify ideas, thoughts, and feelings" (CCSS.ELA-LITERACY.SL.2.5). At the middle school level, students must be able to "include multimedia components (e.g., graphics, images, music, sound) and visual displays in presentations to clarify information" (CCSS.ELA-LITERACY.SL.6.5), while at the high school level "make strategic use of digital media (e.g., textual, graphical, audio, visual, and interactive elements) in presentations to enhance understanding of findings, reasoning, and evidence and to add interest" (CCSS.ELA-LITERACY.SL.11-12.5).

While the intensity and level of Bloom's taxonomy is grade-level dependent, each of these Common Core standards has in common the expectation that all K–12 students will communicate their ideas through multiple multimedia formats, requiring the use of a wide range of technology (Bloom's Taxonomy, n.d.). There are many ways to modify and redesign tasks related to the Common Core State Standards in these areas. Students can use Storybird's digital authoring software to allow students to choose imagery and graphics to create stories and poems. Students can add text to the stories, thus, communicating their ideas. To share widely, students can use the online sharing tool within Storybird to trade stories, comment on other stories, and receive feedback on their stories. Teachers have the option to have students create stories across all academic curriculums, and literacy development can be a co-focus area.

Here are some other practical modification tech strategies to support communicating effectively:

- Use OneNote to combine drafting narrative text, inserting photos, taking screenshots to communicate and share ideas.
- Instead of relying solely on words, use Skitch by Evernote to communicate visual ideas and provide annotations to help direct the audience's attention on the most salient points.
- Facilitate classroom lectures in a flipped style by using Nearpod to communicate lessons and allow students to communicate back and share their learning.

Tech strategy: Videoconference to communicate across cultures (SAMR level: Redefinition). Technology enables students and teachers to communicate with a broader audience, from a classroom within the same school to a classroom in another country. Within the subskill of communicating clearly, the Partnership for 21st Century Learning expects students to communicate in diverse environments. Students who are considered college and career ready in the area of English language arts should "actively seek to understand other perspectives and cultures through reading and listening, and they are able to communicate effectively with people of varied backgrounds" (Common Core State Standards Initiative, 2015). Using a videoconferencing tool such as Skype or Google Hangouts provides opportunities for teachers and students to communicate across cultures. Because this would not have been possible without the use of technology, these videoconferencing tools redefine learning. Prior to the videoconferencing sessions, students from both cultures could research the other students' culture and design questions that arise through this research. During the videoconference, students can have conversations and communicate with each other while learning how to understand other perspectives and cultures. To extend this activity, the students could be placed in small cross-cultural groups and work virtually to create a multimedia presentation describing their experience, common bonds, differences, and reflections.

Here are some other practical redefinition tech strategies to support communicating effectively:

- Use Google Apps for Education to collaboratively research and share research. Other helpful tools are Notability, Evernote, and Keynote.
- Ask students to create informational videos using YouTube or iMovie.
- Have students use voice-recorded technology such as VoiceThread or Knovio to create a presentation on a course topic and then share and allow for peer and teacher feedback.

Reflection Questions for Individual and Group Discussion with Teachers

- How have you used technology to facilitate communication between students, colleagues, and families?
- What parts of the communication process do you think you could augment with technology to change the essential function?

- What best practices can you recommend to teachers interested in the facilitation of building students' ability to effectively communicate as 21st century learners?
- In what ways do your students have opportunities to clearly articulate their ideas, thoughts, and opinions?
- How might being in diverse environments impact communication, and how can technology be used to ameliorate this?
- What forums do you provide for students to demonstrate and document their utilization of various technologies to communicate?
- How and what type of technology can you use to support students in developing listening skills?

Collaboration: Teaming with Teachers and Partnering with Peers

Alone we can do so little; together we can do so much.

—Helen Keller

The ability to work in collaborative teams with a variety of people from different cultural backgrounds and ways of thinking is instrumental to shared ownership and community in schools. Learning activities in schools are certainly "intellectual endeavors." According to Frey, Fisher, and Gonzalez

(2013), "collaborative learning is more than talking and listening to one another; students also need to interact with the content" (p. 221). Having a technology program in place facilitates that process. According to ISTE (2007), students must "use digital media and environments to communicate and work collaboratively, including at a distance, to support individual learning and contribute to learning of others." Technology can be used as a clear pathway to the facilitation of collaborative opportunities that ultimately impact learning.

Mobile technology has increased the different ways in which students and teachers can collaborate with one another. Teachers must provide these opportunities through structured and meaningful technology integration. It is now possible to work on a project with a peer at a school in another city, state, or country without physically meeting. When students have opportunities to work with others, share ideas, and ultimately put them together, they produce a strong product and expand their learning happens. Collaboration is also fun! There is something exciting about working with others, especially while in school. Technology can be used to facilitate this process allowing students to work with more people, share more knowledge, and improve learning capacity while meeting learning objectives.

Practical Tips to Meet the 21st Century Skill of Collaboration with the Use of Technology

Students need many opportunities to practice and master the skill of collaboration by interacting and working with others. The P21 Framework described the 21st century learner as being able to work with others in diverse settings, capable of being flexible and open-minded, as well as contributing fairly to collaborative efforts. Collaboration is also an important component of career and college readiness, and the Common Core standards provide this anchor standard: "Prepare for and participate effectively in a range of conversations and collaborations with diverse partners, building on others' ideas and expressing their own clearly and persuasively" (CCSS.ELA-Literacy.CCRA.SL.1).

From early childhood through high school, students can benefit from opportunities to work with partners or in small or whole groups. If classrooms consist of open dialogue and discussion, students will learn how to work with others both inside and outside the classroom setting. Teachers can model collaborative skills by working with families, administrators, and coworkers. Schools can encourage collaboration by creating an inclusive and welcoming environment for all and supporting teachers who are flexible, open-minded, and collaborative. How can technology provide even greater ways for collaboration to occur? This next section will provide technology strategies from augmentation to redefinition.

Subskill: Collaborate with Others

Collaboration is an essential skill that has been focused on in some capacity in the Common Core State Standards, the ISTE Standards for Students, and the P21 Framework. Collaboration allows for a deeper understanding of content while working with others and developing solutions to problems (Beers, 2011). As a critical 21st century skill, collaboration is developed through educators (Okada, Rabello, & Ferreira, 2014). The Partnership for 21st Century Learning defines "to collaborate with others" as having the ability to

- Demonstrate ability to work effectively and respectfully with diverse teams.

- Exercise flexibility and willingness to be helpful in making necessary compromises to accomplish a common goal.

- Assume shared responsibility for collaborative work, and value the individual contributions made by each team member. (2015, p. 4)

Technology provides endless ideas and examples teachers and students can use to prompt creative thought and to collaborate with one another. Below are specific technology strategies shared with the goal of moving from using technology to collaborate as a substitute to ways of augmenting, modifying, and redefining ways to collaborate.

Tech strategy: Create a class wiki to collaborate with others (SAMR level: Augmentation). In order to allow greater collaboration outside of the classroom setting, technology tools such as wikis allow students to share and work together in a 24/7 learning environment. A teacher can create a wiki for a specific course with separate pages for course topics. Direct students to add to each page of the wiki and contribute a related resource that every student can access. This type of collaboration can be done in the classroom if students are asked to share resources they found with their classmates, but technology makes the process easier and more efficient. Wikispaces and Google Sites are free to educators and user friendly. The wiki can serve as evidence of student learning and be accessed even after the course is over. This type of tool also allows students to see each other's work and share ideas freely. Students can build on each other's work as they collaborate to create their course wiki.

Here are some other practical augmentation tech strategies to encourage collaboration:

- Use a shared document tool (e.g., Google Docs, Evernote, Padlet) where students can collaborate with each other by combining their ideas to develop a final end product.
- Students collaborate with one another regarding a course topic. They can participate and develop new ideas though virtual sharing sessions within a course learning system (e.g., Blackboard Collaborate, Adobe Connect, Google Hangouts).
- Create groups and give each group a hashtag to identify their group. The groups would then be assigned something to research and a cause to share with others. The groups would collaborate and find information on their topic. They would then use a social media tool (such as Twitter) and share the resources using their group hashtag.

Tech strategy: Develop Personal Learning Networks and study groups to collaborate with others (SAMR level: Modification). With the multitude of social media and networking opportunities available, students can benefit from learning how to use these tools for educational reasons and also learning how to collaborate. Teachers and students can develop Personal Learning Networks (PLN) and online study groups to provide 24/7 connected learning with others and opportunities to problem solve collectively on course content. Ask students to keep an online journal of the many ways they interact online and how this contributes to their learning. They can also comment on their peers' journals. Students can use a visual tool like Prezi or Bubbl. us to create a representation of their PLN or study group. Students within the class will follow each other, help each other gain followers, and collaborate within the PLN and study group. In addition, students can collaborate through ePals and work on projects with other students across the world. This would broaden their PLN and study group to work with students beyond the context of their own school, community, and country. Some tools to use to collaborate within PLNS and study groups are Flowdock, Thinkbinder, Groupboard, Twiddla, and Pinterest.

Here are some other practical modification tech strategies to encourage collaboration:

- Student teams work collaboratively to compile similar topics on a webmix, using an application such as Symbaloo.
- Create an EDUblog classroom account and have the students join the class, and then blog about course related information. Students will also use a

whiteboard app (e.g., EduCreations, Flowboard, Web Whiteboard, Simple Surface) to collaborate within their groups, and then share on their blogs and respond to classmate blogs as well.

- Student teams collaborate and create a presentation using an online tool of their choice (e.g., VoiceThread, Prezi, Google Slides).

Tech strategy: Co-create and share digital stories with a partner school in another country (SAMR level: Redefinition). Given the competitive nature of our digital society, it is imperative that teachers prepare citizens who are able to work collaboratively, can communicate effectively with diverse populations, and possess problem-solving skills (Reed, n.d.). Students can be assigned small groups, and then within these groups, they can use digital video or storytelling tools to co-create a presentation about a course topic. The more the project is applicable to real life, the more meaningful the assignment. These tools can help students use digital tools to co-create and share information about their communities with students in partner schools (Reed, n.d.). This project reaches the redefinition level when it is shared with others outside the school community such as a partner school.

Here are some other practical redefinition tech strategies to encourage collaboration:

- In small groups, students co-create a digital book or movie and co-publish this work on the Internet for others to see. Possible tools include WattPad, iMovie, and YouTube.

- Connect students from different cultures, provide opportunities for students to research and ask questions and collaborate with one another. Possible tools include Google Hangouts and Skype.
- Problem-based learning provides opportunities for collaboration and connection to real life problems. Students could blog about their experiences with the online community.

Reflection Questions for Individual and Group Discussion with Teachers

- How can you use technology to foster immersive group project experiences?
- What are some of the largest challenges with collaboration that technology can help ameliorate?
- In what ways can you use technology to track contributions in collaborative efforts?
- In what ways have you already been successful with using technology for group assignment?
- How have you used technology to collaborate with teachers in co-planning?
- What specific functionalities do you look for in apps geared towards facilitating collaboration?

Creativity: Encouraging Innovation and Invention

Make an empty space in any corner of your mind, and creativity will instantly fill it.

—Dee Hock

Teachers, administrators, and schools play an important role when supporting an environment of creativity, innovation, and invention. The ISTE Standards for Students related to creativity and innovation include "demonstrate creative thinking, construct knowledge, and develop innovative products and processes using technology" (ISTE, 2007). When students have tools and the ability to make choices for how they will use these tools to demonstrate their knowledge and thinking, innovation and invention flourishes. Teachers should be encouraged and allowed to take risks so they can use their expertise to create collaborative and creative environments for students (Moczygemba, 2014; Ryshke, 2012). As districts move along the SAMR ladder within their technology program, the ultimate goal is for teachers and students to use technology to create new tasks and redefine teaching and learning.

The 21st century skill of creativity and innovation shifts learning from teacher-centered to student-centered. Levinson (2010) explained:

Technology has flipped our roles. It used to be that parents and teachers taught children. Now the reverse is also true, and the quicker we grasp this concept, the better we will all be to live in the 21st century. (pp. 35–36)

Students are expected to think creatively, work creatively with others, and implement innovation (National Education Association, 2014). In addition, if teachers are expected to encourage innovation and invention, they need opportunities and time to become learners as well (Frey et al., 2013). This section includes specific ways to use technology to encourage innovation and invention. We will also suggest ways teachers can be supported to take risks and try out new tools within their teaching and learning environment.

Practical Tips to Meet the 21st Century Skill of Creativity with the Use of Technology

To *think creatively* and *implement innovations* are sub-skill areas that the P21 Framework has identified as critical for 21st century learners. Teachers must provide students with the chance to think, create, and refine new ideas. Abdi and Rostami (2012) asserted "people have to improve their creative thinking in order to develop technological improvements and utilize that in today's continuously changing and developing world" (p. 105). Providing students with choice in assignments and assessments demonstrates to teachers they have mastered the learning objectives. Instead of having students take a test or write a paper, allow their creativity to spark and give them the autonomy and creative license to produce tangibles demonstrating their learning while being engaged and having fun. Instead of reading stories to students from beginning to end, read half, and then allow them to think of an ending. This can occur in classes that are designed provide learning opportunities and engagement activities that activate students' multiple intelligences and identify their processes of creativity (Clarke & Cripps, 2012). Technology is one area that has served as a catalyst to demonstrating the results of creative minds. Below you will find several instructional strategies and learning activities to foster students' creativity while augmenting, modifying, and redefining technology usage in the classroom.

Subskill: Think Creatively

Creative potential flourishes when students have opportunities to think creatively. Creativity can be assessed by looking at whether something is original, flexible, fluent, appropriate, and relevant (Edwards, 2010). Teachers can facilitate creative potential by providing divergent thinking and activities that are open-ended within the classroom. In addition, focusing on the *process* instead of the *product* will allow students to be creative. Using differentiation strategies such as tic tac toe boards and choice boards help students think about how they will demonstrate their learning. Students need activities and materials that require them to explore and think (Mayesky, 2012). In order to encourage creative thinking within classrooms, teachers should understand and value creativity. A creative teacher is able to understand the perspective of students and integrates assignments or topics students are interested in (Henriksen & Mishra, 2013). Technology provides endless ideas and examples teachers and students can use to prompt creative thought. Below are specific technology strategies shared with the goal of moving from using technology as a substitute to redefining learning:

Tech strategy: Use mind mapping and brainstorming sessions to inspire creative thinking (SAMR level: Augmentation). Brainstorming helps to promote creativity as an idea generator (Treffinger, 2008). Mind mapping creates a visual map of ideas and thoughts, also encouraging creativity and critical thinking. Providing students with activities that are divergent such as brainstorming and mind mapping allows for flexibility, risk-taking, and helps to build confidence, all skills that are necessary to succeed in a global society. There are many online tools that can help facilitate this process. For example, Popplet is a free tool that allows students to create mind maps and brainstorm. Mindmeister can also be used as a tool for brainstorming. Students and teachers can share their thoughts and ideas in a collaborative way.

Here are some other practical augmentation tech strategies to encourage creative thinking. Ask students to

- Create digital posters using Glogster.
- Embed digital photos and texts using Prezi.
- Create interactive timelines using Timetoast.

Tech strategy: Allow students to choose digital tools or resources to encourage creative thinking (SAMR level: Modification). One ISTE standard for teachers is to facilitate and inspire student learning and creativity (2008). When students are given the choice to decide on the task they will complete, how they will accomplish the task, and the tools they will use, students are motivated and encouraged to think creatively. Students are able to "elaborate, refine, analyze and evaluate their own ideas in order to improve and maximize creative effort" (Partnership for 21st Century Learning, 2015). If students have a choice, they can use tools they are comfortable with and most likely create more meaningful work.

Students need opportunities to explore real-world problems and develop solutions using digital tools (ISTE, 2007). When students can choose a topic that pertains to them, this can help them become advocates and problem solvers in addition to being creative thinkers. Also, one student may find using Notability helpful while another one prefers to use OneNote or VoiceThread. Allowing students to decide what tool to use prompts creativity. This blog lists 18 apps that support creativity: www.edutopia.org/blog/apps-for-creativity-diane-darrow. The choices are endless.

Here are some other practical modification tech strategies to encourage creative thinking. Students can

- Showcase their work by creating infographics using tools such as Easel.ly or Piktochart.

- Use screencasting tools to prompt creative thinking such as Screenr, Camstudio, or iMovie.
- Record ideas and sound using EduCreations.

Tech strategy: Create a makerspace to inspire creative thinking (SAMR level: Redefinition). Makerspaces are becoming common in many schools and libraries. A makerspace, in its simplest form, is a dedicated space with tools, equipment, and technology where individuals can create and collaborate on various projects (Schrock, 2014). Schools can develop a makerspace by designating a physical space where students have access to tools and technology to create. A makerspace can also be virtual where students use technology to create innovative projects. Teachers can come together to develop a makerspace area for students, or part of a collaborative project can involve students and teachers in creating the actual makerspace. Makerspaces can be different and tailored to the individual needs and interests of the students in your school. The types of projects created within a makerspace are infinite as it encourages creativity.

The purpose of a makerspace is to provide students with opportunities to have hands-on experiences and be creators instead of consumers. Since many of the creations can be shared outside of the school setting with the use of technology, this helps to redefine learning. The MakerEd website has many ideas for student creations. The diverse ideas located in the project gallery (e.g., a bike light, cupcake oven, and cloud lamp) demonstrate why including a makerspace would inspire creative thinking and how the creations can be showcased and shared to a broad audience.

Here are some other practical redefinition tech strategies to encourage creative thinking. Encourage students to

- Code and create their own website for a cause that is important to them. What they create can then be shared with a broader audience.
- Engage in robotics, which will foster their engineering, science, math, and problem-solving skills. The student creations can be shared with a virtual community. Examples of useful tools are Bee-Bot, RobotBASIC, EZ-Robot, and LEGO Robotics.
- Create interactive 3-D timelines to focus on a variety of historical, life, and legal events. They can publish the timelines online and analyze them for historical correctness. Examples of useful tools are Tiki-Toki, Timeglider, and Timetoast.

Subskill: Implement Innovations

Given the fact that we live in a changing world, it is pertinent that teachers help students develop and implement innovations. The Partnership for 21st Century Learning (2015, p. 4) suggests students not only think creatively but also "act on creative ideas to make a tangible and useful contribution to the field in which the innovation will occur." In order for students and teachers to be innovative, they must feel safe and supported within the learning environment.

Strategies such as problem-based learning, group work, and student-led projects help foster innovation. Failure should be looked at as a positive step toward innovation, and this attitude encourages risk-taking (Ryshke, 2012).

Technology use is imperative when preparing students to be competent and competitive in a global society. However, technology is mostly being used at the substitution level as described by the following executive summary:

> Right now, schools use technology primarily as a tool for developing students' computer and Internet skills. This is important, but technology proficiency is simply the point of entry to the digital world— and it is only a small sliver of the far-reaching utility of technology as a powerful enabling tool for a full range of essential knowledge and skills. ("Maximizing the Impact," 2007, p. 3)

Teachers can and must use technology past the substitution stage to encourage innovation and prepare 21st century learners. Districts, administrators, and teachers can encourage risk-taking and innovation by taking a risk and supporting those who also take risks when it comes to implementing innovations.

Tech strategy: Provide examples and model for students—Implementing innovations (SAMR level: Augmentation). Students may want to be innovative but do not know how. Teachers need to be open to implementing innovations themselves to serve as a model for their students. For example, teachers could take a risk and try out a new technology or tool within the classroom setting. Talk to the students about how you are taking a risk and trying something new. Students can learn from this experience ways they can also implement innovations. Encourage students to continue to try even if they encounter failure. This video demonstrates this concept: www.youtube.com/watch?v=zLYECIjmnQs

Here are some other practical augmentation tech strategies to implement innovations:

- Share stories of how children implement innovations. Here is a great video to share (Audri's Rube Goldberg Monster Trap): https://www.youtube.com/watch?v=0uDDEEHDf1Y.
- Allow students to create projects digitally. The tools can be organized in a webmix tool such as Symbaloo.
- Use online technology to help spark innovative thinking like videos and pictures.

Tech strategy: Build case studies and problem-based learning opportunities for innovative thinking (SAMR level: Modification). The Partnership for 21st Century Learning has a program called Exemplar Schools, which highlights best practices in preparing 21st century learners. The case studies can be found here: www.p21.org/exemplar-program-case-studies. The Meadowbrook School in Massachusetts created an innovation lab called Eureka Lab. The Eureka Lab is a physical place and an idea (see www.eureka-lab.org). Within the lab, there are multiple technology tools students and teachers can use to modify learning and implement innovations moving up the SAMR ladder. Even if a school does not have space for a physical lab, teachers can create a small space in the classroom designated for innovations, or the lab can exist in the cloud where students have access to resources and tools to assist them in innovative design. Adding a few technology tools, such as 3-D printers and digital cameras, within a classroom setting can help students explore and create innovations. In addition, a variety of real life case studies and project-based learning opportunities should be available to students. Innovative 21st century learning is student-directed, collaborative, and interactive, and it is not confined within the four walls of a classroom.

Here are some other practical modification tech strategies to implement innovations. Provide opportunities for students to

- Interview experts on course topics through the use of videoconferencing tools such Skype, Adobe Connect, ZOOMHD, GoToMeeting, and WebEx. These virtual meetings will help generate ideas for students and help with the innovation process.
- Use interactive video tools to watch videos created by their teachers or experts in the field so that they can edit and engage with video and share their creations. Examples of tools to use include TED-Ed, eduCanon, EDPuzzle, and Zaption.
- Design and share presentations based on real life problems and cases using tools such as Keynote, PowToon Studio, Prezi, #Slides, and Google Slides.

- Create an assigned end product using a format that they choose. For example, a geographic model of their favorite city. Provide tools for creative thinking, innovation, and practice such as SketchUp to help get students ideas going. Include a reflective component where students document their process, and make changes based on what they have created.

Tech strategy: Provide 3-D geographic topology landscapes and terrain models (SAMR level: Redefinition). Technology enables the production of tangible visual representations that were once not available. Within the area of creativity and innovation, the Partnership for 21st Century Learning (2015) explains that in order for contributions to the field to be useful, students must bring creative ideas to fruition. Technology gives students the opportunity to bring their creative ideas to life by developing a product. Students can bring their ideas to life using 3-D printers. In a geography class, using 3-D printers gives students the chance to explore elements of the earth in a new and exciting way. They can closely explore terrain models and elements of the earth including tundra, mountain, rivers, and ecosystems.

Here are some other practical redefinition tech strategies to implement innovations. Ask students to

- Use LaserOrigami (a rapid prototyping system used to create 3-D objects with a laser cutter) to produce prototypes of objects created in STEM classes. Examples can be found here: http://hpi.de/baudisch/projects/laserorigami.html.

- Use SketchUp to create 3-D diagrams and models with specified dimensions and blueprinting elements.
- Freely construct and engineer whatever their creative minds bring to physical fruition in a makerspace laboratory you have developed.

Reflection Questions for Individual and Group Discussion with Teachers

- What can we do or do we do to encourage innovation for faculty and students?
- What are you doing that works?
- What innovative techniques do you use to improve student learning?
- What kind of opportunities do you have to be innovative and creative?
- How do students showcase their work and what kind of tools do they use?
- In what ways do you receive support when it comes to trying something new or being innovative?
- How do you facilitate and inspire student creativity?

To give your feedback on this publication and be entered into a drawing for a free ASCD Arias e-book, please visit **www.ascd.org/ariasfeedback**

ENCORE

TOOLS AND RESOURCES

The Encore section includes the **Action Plan for Leveraging Technology and the 4Cs,** which offers a way for teachers to record and document their ideas, reflect on their experiences, and share what they are doing with their peers and administrators. You can also download the document in Google Docs: http://tinyurl.com/actionplan4cs or contact us directly (see p. 57) if you have any issues. Additional practical tools are available online:

- **Share Your Story with Us: How Do You Integrate the 4Cs?** Please feel free to share your own story or stories on ways you integrate technology and the 4Cs and complete our short survey: http://goo.gl/forms/ BCsCbnQBY6. We intend to share these stories in future publications.

- **Graphic Organizer for App Choice and Alignment with 4Cs**. Use this graphic organizer to categorize and align the apps you are using with one of the 4Cs: http://tinyurl.com/TechTools21stcenturytemplate.

- **Leveraging Technology to Integrate the 4Cs Wiki**. We created an example of a wiki to show how technology can increase collaboration and creativity: http://leveragingtechnologytointegratethe4cs. wikispaces.com/. We hope that you will join our wiki, add to it, or use the posted resources.

Action Plan for Leveraging Technology and the 4Cs

Describe ideas or ways you do or will use technology to foster one of the 4Cs (Critical Thinking, Communication, Collaboration, and Creativity):

Actions steps you will take to accomplish this goal (include what, why, when, and how):

What challenges do you foresee?

What supports and resources do you need to accomplish your goals?

Reflection:

Additional notes and comments:

References

Abdi, A., & Rostami, M. (2012). The effect multiple intelligences-based instruction on students' creative thinkingability at 5th grade in primary school. *Social and Behavioral Sciences, 47,* 105–108.

Bain, K. (n.d.). Fostering critical thinking with technology. Best Teacher Institute Inc. South Orange, NJ. http://www.bestteachersinstitute.org/id98.html

Beers, S. Z. (2011). *Teaching 21st century skills: An ASCD action tool.* Alexandria, VA: ASCD.

Bloom, B. S. (Ed.). (1956). *Taxonomy of educational objectives: The classification of educational goals: Handbook I. Cognitive domain.* New York: David McKay Company, Inc.

Bloom's Taxonomy (n.d.). Bloom's taxonomy questions. http://www.bloomstaxonomy.org/Blooms%20Taxonomy%20questions.pdf

Chick, N. (n.d.). Metacognition: Thinking about one's thinking. Vanderbilt University. Center for Teaching. http://cft.vanderbilt.edu/guides-sub-pages/metacognition/

Clark, L. (2014). Systems thinking: Promoting critical thinking in the early years. http://www.p21.org/news-events/p21blog/1434-systems-thinking-promoting-critical-

Clarke, A., & Cripps, P. (2012). Fostering creativity: A multiple intelligences approach to designing learning in undergraduate fine art. *International Journal of Art & Design Education, 31*(2), 113-126. doi:10.1111/j.1476-8070.2012.01736.x

Common Core State Standards Initiative (2015). Read the standards. http://www.corestandards.org/

Edwards, L. (2010). *The creative arts: A process approach for teachers and children* (5th ed.). Pearson Education.

Frey, N., Fisher, D., & Gonzalez, A. (2013). *Teaching with tablets: How do I integrate tablets with effective instruction?* Alexandria, VA: ASCD.

Gray, S. (2012). Technology helps students find comfort in the classroom. Getting Smart. http://gettingsmart.com/2012/09/technology-helps-students-find-comfort-in-classroom/

Green, L. S. (2014). Through the looking glass. *Knowledge Quest, 43*(1), 36-43. International Society for Technology of Education (2014). ISTE Standards for Students. http://www.iste.org/docs/pdfs/20-14_ISTE_ Standards-S_PDF.pdf.

Henriksen, D., & Mishra, P. (2013). Learning from creative teachers. *Educational Leadership, 70*(5). http://www.ascd.org/publications/ educational-leadership/

International Society for Technology of Education. (2007). ISTE Standards for Students. http://www.iste.org/docs/pdfs/20-14_ISTE_Standards-S_PDF.pdf

International Society for Technology in Education. (2008). ISTE Standards for Teachers. http://www.iste.org/standards/ISTE-standards/ standards-for-teachers

Johnson, D. (2013). Power up! Teaching above the line. *Educational Leadership, 71*(4), 84–87.

Levinson, M. (2010). *From fear to Facebook: One school's journey.* Eugene, OR: International Society for Technology in Education.

Luterbach, K. J., & Brown, C. (2011). Education for the 21st century. *International Journal of Applied Educational Studies, 10*(2), 14–32.

MacKnight, C. (2000). Teaching critical thinking through online discussions. *Educause Quarterly 4.* http://net.educause.edu/ir/library/pdf/ eqm0048.pdf

Maximizing the impact: The pivotal role of technology in a 21st century education system. (2007). Eugene, OR: International Society for Technology in Education; Glen Burnie, MD: State Educational Technology Directors Association; Tucson, AZ: Partnership for 21st Century Skills. http://www.p21.org/storage/documents/p21setdaistepaper.pdf

Mayesky, M. (2012). *Creative activities for young children.* Belmont, CA: Wadsworth Cengage Learning.

Mobile learning: A genie on the loose. (2013). *Educational Leadership, 70*(6), 8.

Moczygemba, R. (2014). If you can flip a classroom, you can flip a district. *International Society for Technology of Education.* http://www.iste.org.

National Education Association. (2014). Preparing 21st century students for a global society: An educator's guide to the "Four Cs." http://www. nea.org/assets/docs/A-Guide-to-Four-Cs.pdf

National Governors Association Center for Best Practices & Council of Chief State School Officers. (2010). *Common Core State Standards for English Language Arts & Literacy in History/Social Studies, Science, and Technical Subjects.* Washington, DC: Author.

Okada, A., Rabello, C. & Ferreira, G. (2014). Developing 21st century skills through colearning with OER and social networks. In: European distance and e-earning network 2014 research workshop, 27-28 October 2014, Oxford, UK, European Distance and E- Learning Network, pp. 121–130.

Partnership for 21st Century Learning. (2015). P21 framework definitions. http://www.p21.org/storage/documents/docs/P21_Framework_Definitions_New_Logo_2015.pdf

Personalized learning boosts STEM interest, survey says. (2012). *American School & University, 84*(10), 10.

Pi-Hsia, H., Gwo-Jen, H., Yueh-Hsun, L., Tsung-Hsun, W., Vogel, B., Milrad, M., & Johansson, E. (2014). A problem-based ubiquitous learning approach to improving the questioning abilities of elementary school students. *Journal of Educational Technology & Society, 17*(4), 316-334.

Puentedura, R. (2009). As we may teach. Educational technology, from theory to practice. http://www.hippasus.com/

Reed, J. (n.d.). Global collaboration and learning. *Ed Tech Magazine.* Retrieved from http://www.edtechmagazine.com/k12/article/2007/09/global-collaboration-and-learning

Richardson, W. (2010). *Blogs, wikis, podcasts, and other powerful web tools for classrooms* (3rd ed.). Thousand Oaks, CA: Corwin.

Rosefsky Saavedra, A., & Opfer, V. D. (2012). Learning 21st-century skills requires 21st century teaching. *Phi Delta Kappan, 94*(2), 8–13.

Ryshke, R. (2012). What schools can do to encourage innovation. Extracted from http://rryshke.wordpress.com/2012/02/26/what-schools-can-do-to-encourage-innovation/

Schrock, A. R. (2014). Education in disguise: Culture of a hacker and maker space. *InterActions: UCLA Journal of Education and Information Studies, 10*(1), 1–25.

Treffinger, D. (2008). Preparing creative and critical thinkers. *Educational Leadership, 65.* http://www.ascd.org/publications/educational-leadership/summer08/vol65/num09/Preparing-Creative-and-Critical-Thinkers.aspx

You, C. A. R., & Richman, P. (2014). Improving learning through family–school partnerships. *Leadership, 44*(1), 12–15.

Related Resources

At the time of publication, the following ASCD resources were available (ASCD stock numbers appear in parentheses). For up-to-date information about ASCD resources, go to www.ascd.org. You can search the complete archives of *Educational Leadership* at http://www.ascd.org/el.

ASCD EDge®
Exchange ideas and connect with other educators interested in technology and the 4Cs on the social networking site ASCD EDge at http://ascdedge.ascd.org.

Print Products
Digital Learning Strategies: How do I assign and assess 21st century work? (ASCD Arias) by Michael Fisher (#SF114045)

Getting Started with Blended Learning: How do I integrate online and face-to-face Instruction? (ASCD Arias) by William Kist (#SF115073)

Teaching 21st Century Skills: An ASCD Action Tool by Sue Z. Beers (#111021)

Teaching with Tablets: How do I integrate tablets with effective instruction? (ASCD Arias) by Nancy Frey, Doug Fisher, & Alex Gonzalez (#SF113074)

ASCD PD Online® Courses
Blended Learning: An Introduction (#PD14OC009)

From Vision to Action: The 21st Century Teaching and Learning Plan (#PD11OC126M)

Technology in Schools: A Balanced Perspective, 2nd edition (#PD11OC109)

For more information: send e-mail to member@ascd.org; call 1-800-933-2723 or 703-578-9600, press 2; send a fax to 703-575-5400; or write to Information Services, ASCD, 1703 N. Beauregard St., Alexandria, VA 22311-1714 USA.

About the Authors

Stephanie Smith Budhai, PhD, is an assistant professor and director of graduate education at Neumann University, holding a PhD in Learning Technologies and certification as a K–12 Instructional Technology Specialist from the Pennsylvania Department of Education. She recently developed a state approved program to prepare K–12 teachers to design, deliver, and assess learning in online modalities. She has published articles surrounding the use of technology in education, and her research and practical experience has surrounded online and blended learning, assistive technology in the K–12 classroom, and pre-service teacher development. Stephanie has experience as an itinerant special education teacher, supplemental education teacher, and behavior specialist. She can be reached at budhais@neumann.edu.

Laura McLaughlin Taddei, EdD, is a leader in higher education with a mix of administrative and teaching responsibilities and is currently an assistant professor of Education at Neumann University. She is a professional development speaker in both higher education and preK–12 settings. Her education career began teaching in the early childhood classroom, preK–4, and then transitioned into providing interactive professional development geared toward teacher and institutional needs. Laura's research interests are in the area of teacher and faculty development, instructional coaching, culturally responsive teaching, building community within classrooms and institutions, and educational technology. She can be reached at taddeil@neumann.edu.

Printed in January 2022
by Rotomail Italia S.p.A., Vignate (MI) - Italy